APPLE A DAY

Especially for:

_____

ISBN: 1-56245-019-0

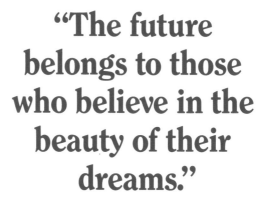

"The future belongs to those who believe in the beauty of their dreams."

— ELEANOR ROOSEVELT

"Accept the challenges, so that you may feel the exhilaration of victory."

— GENERAL GEORGE S. PATTON

"We are
continually
faced by great
opportunities
brilliantly
disguised as
insolvable
problems."

"Do not follow where the path may lead . . . . Go instead where there is no path and leave a trail."

"Well done is better than well said."

— BEN FRANKLIN

"The greatest
thing in this world
is not so much
where we are, but
in what direction
we are moving."

— O.W. HOLMES

"Make the
mistakes of
yesterday your
lessons for
today."

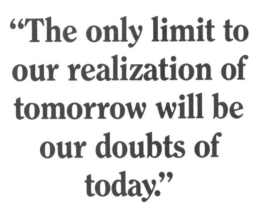

"The only limit to our realization of tomorrow will be our doubts of today."

— FRANKLIN D. ROOSEVELT

"When nothing seems to help,
I go and look at a stonecutter
hammering away at his rock
perhaps a hundred times
without as much as a crack
showing in it. Yet at the
hundred and first blow it will
spilt in two, and I know it was
not that blow that did it — but
all that had gone before."

— JACOB RIIS

> "It is a funny thing about life; if you refuse to accept anything but the best, you very often get it."

— SOMERSET MAUGHAM

"Act as though it were impossible to fail."

> **"Destiny is not a matter of chance; it is a matter of choice."**

"Unless you try to do something beyond what you have already mastered, you will never grow."

— RALPH WALDO EMERSON

"If you've made
up your mind
you can do
something, you're
absolutely right."

"The difference between the impossible and the possible lies in a person's determination."

— TOMMY LASORDA
Major League Manager

"We cannot direct
the wind . . .
but we can adjust
the sails."

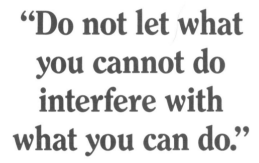

"Do not let what you cannot do interfere with what you can do."

— JOHN WOODEN
College Basketball Coach

"Failure is not
the worst thing
in the world.
The very worst is
not to try."

"Success is a
journey, not a
destination."

— BEN SWEETLAND

"Inch by inch,
life's a cinch.

Yard by yard,
life is hard."

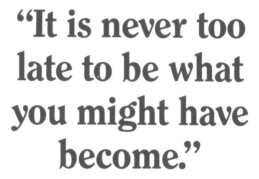

"It is never too late to be what you might have become."

— GEORGE ELIOT

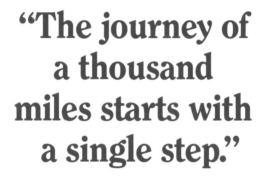

"The journey of a thousand miles starts with a single step."

— CHINESE PROVERB

"Good intentions
are no substitute
for action; failure
usually follows
the path of least
persistence."

"People can alter
their lives by
altering their
attitudes."

— WILLIAM JAMES

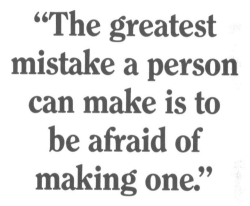

"The greatest mistake a person can make is to be afraid of making one."

— ELBERT HUBBARD

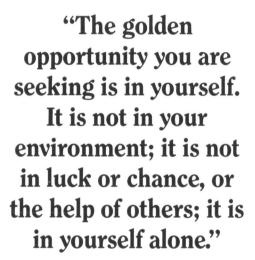

"The golden opportunity you are seeking is in yourself. It is not in your environment; it is not in luck or chance, or the help of others; it is in yourself alone."

— ORISON SWETT MARDEN

"Failure
is success
if we learn
from it."

— MALCOLM S. FORBES

"Don't wait for your ship to come in; swim out to it."

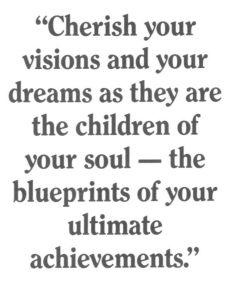

"Cherish your
visions and your
dreams as they are
the children of
your soul — the
blueprints of your
ultimate
achievements."

— NAPOLEON HILL

"In the middle of difficulty lies opportunity."

— ALBERT EINSTEIN

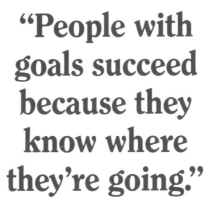

"People with goals succeed because they know where they're going."

— EARL NIGHTINGALE

"Keep trying.
It's only from
the valley that
the mountain
seems high."

"The price of success is perseverance. The price of failure comes cheaper."

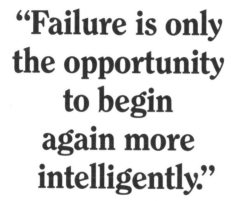

"Failure is only the opportunity to begin again more intelligently."

— HENRY FORD

"One cannot
change yesterday,
but only make the
most of today, and
look with hope
toward tomorrow."

"People rarely
succeed at
anything unless
they have fun
doing it."

"Those who
bring sunshine to
the lives of others
cannot keep it
from themselves."

— JAMES BARRIE

"Most people are
about as happy
as they make
up their minds
to be."

— ABRAHAM LINCOLN

"Happiness is
not the absence
of conflict, but
the ability to cope
with it."

"Whether you think you can or think you can't — you are right."

— HENRY FORD

"The mind, like a parachute, functions only when open."

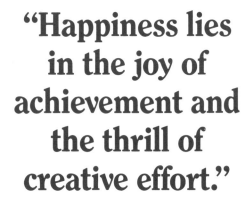

"Happiness lies in the joy of achievement and the thrill of creative effort."

— FRANKLIN ROOSEVELT

"Use the talents you possess, for the woods would be very silent if no birds sang except the best."

"*Did* is a word of
achievement;
Won't is a word of retreat;
Might is a word of
bereavement;
Can't is a word of defeat;
Ought is a word of duty;
Try is a word each hour;
Will is a word of beauty;
Can is a word of power."

"I

Write one
g these
on board

de

t

determines your altitude."

— ZIG ZIGLAR

"You may not have been responsible for your heritage, but you are responsible for your future."

"The difference between ordinary and extraordinary is that little extra."

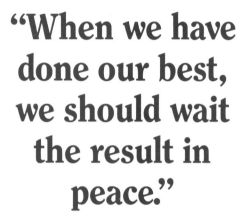

"When we have done our best, we should wait the result in peace."

— J. LUBBOCK

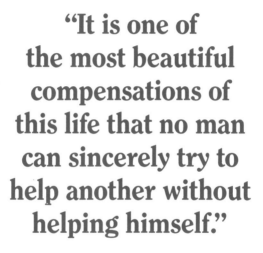

"It is one of
the most beautiful
compensations of
this life that no man
can sincerely try to
help another without
helping himself."

— RALPH WALDO EMERSON

"If a man is called to be a streetsweeper, he should sweep streets even as Michelangelo painted, or Beethoven composed music, or Shakespeare wrote poetry. He should sweep streets so well that all the hosts of heaven and earth will pause to say, here lived a great streetsweeper who did his job well."

— MARTIN LUTHER KING, JR.

"The quality of a
person's life is in direct
proportion to their
commitment to
excellence, regardless
of their chosen field
of endeavor."

— VINCENT T. LOMBARDI

"Genius is the ability to reduce the complicated to the simple."

— C.W. CERAN

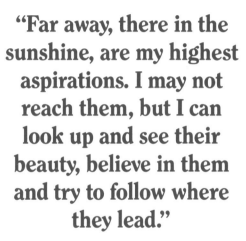

"Far away, there in the sunshine, are my highest aspirations. I may not reach them, but I can look up and see their beauty, believe in them and try to follow where they lead."

— LOUISA MAY ALCOTT

"There's no thrill in easy
sailing when the skies are
clear and blue; there's no joy
in merely doing things
which any one can do. But
there is some satisfaction
that is mighty sweet to take,
when you reach a
destination that you thought
you'd never make."

— SPIRELLA

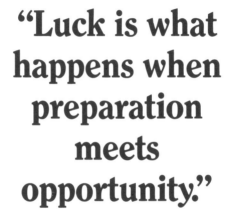

"Luck is what happens when preparation meets opportunity."

— ELMER LETTERMAN

"The harder you work the luckier you get."

— **GARY PLAYER**
Golfer

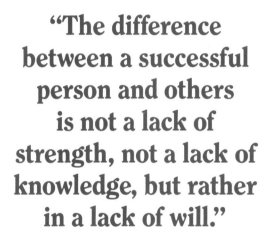

"The difference
between a successful
person and others
is not a lack of
strength, not a lack of
knowledge, but rather
in a lack of will."

— VINCENT T. LOMBARDI

"You must begin
to think of
yourself as
becoming the
person you want
to be."

— DAVID VISCOTT

"Live your life each day as you would climb a mountain. An occasional glance toward the summit keeps the goal in mind, but many beautiful scenes are to be observed from each new vantage point. Climb slowly, steadily, enjoying each passing moment, and the view from the summit will serve as a fitting climax for the journey."

— HAROLD V. MELCHERT

"Obstacles are
what you see
when you take
your eyes off
your goals."

"Aerodynamically the bumble bee shouldn't be able to fly, but the bumble bee doesn't know it so it goes on flying anyway."

— MARY KAY ASH

"No one
can make you
feel inferior
without your
permission."

"When we give it our all, we can live with ourselves — regardless of the results."

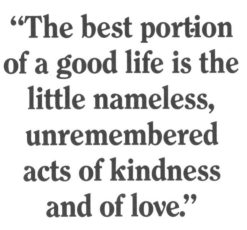

"The best portion
of a good life is the
little nameless,
unremembered
acts of kindness
and of love."

— WILLIAM WORDSWORTH

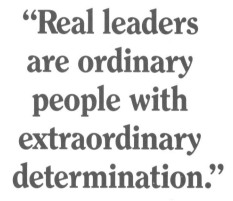

"Real leaders
are ordinary
people with
extraordinary
determination."

"The courage to speak must be matched by the wisdom to listen."

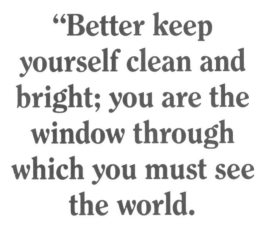

"Better keep
yourself clean and
bright; you are the
window through
which you must see
the world.

— GEORGE BERNARD SHAW

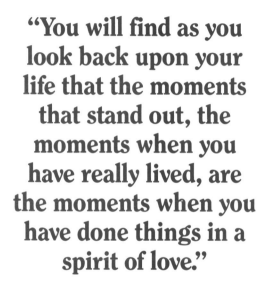

"You will find as you look back upon your life that the moments that stand out, the moments when you have really lived, are the moments when you have done things in a spirit of love."

— HENRY DRUMMOND

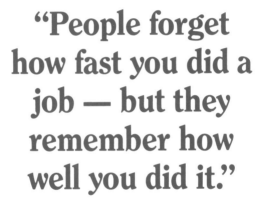

"People forget how fast you did a job — but they remember how well you did it."

— HOWARD W. NEWTON

"**Regardless of your past, your future is a clean slate.**"

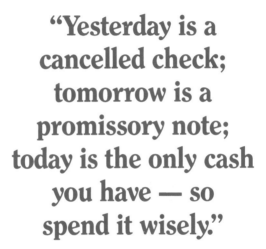

"Yesterday is a cancelled check; tomorrow is a promissory note; today is the only cash you have — so spend it wisely."

— KAY LYONS

"Every job is
a self-portrait
of the person
who did it."

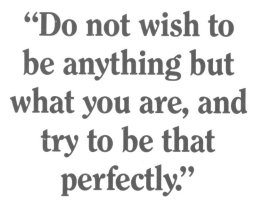

"Do not wish to
be anything but
what you are, and
try to be that
perfectly."

— ST. FRANCIS DE SALES

"Whatever happens, do not lose hold of the two main ropes of life — hope and faith."

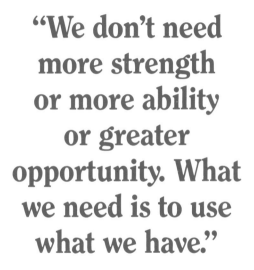

"We don't need
more strength
or more ability
or greater
opportunity. What
we need is to use
what we have."

— BASIL S. WALSH

"It takes both
rain and
sunshine to
make a
rainbow."

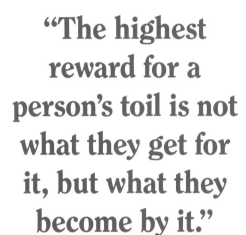

"The highest reward for a person's toil is not what they get for it, but what they become by it."

— JOHN RUSKIN

Other Great Quotations Books:

- The Book of Proverbs
- Aged to Perfection
- Retirement
- Love on Your
  Wedding Day
- Thinking of You
- The Unofficial
  Executive Survival
  Guide
- Inspirations
- Sports Poop
- Over the Hill
- Golf Humor
- Happy Birthday
  to the Golfer
- Stress
- Cat Tales
- The Unofficial Christmas
  Survival Guide

- The Unofficial Survival
  Guide To Parenthood
- A Smile Increases
  Your Face Value
- Keys to Happiness
- Things You'll Learn...
- Teachers Inspirations
- Boyfriends Live
  Longer than...
- Worms of Wisdom
- Our Life Together
- Thoughts from the Heart
- An Apple a Day
- The Joy of Family
- What to Tell Your
  Children
- Proverbs Vol. II
- A Friend is a Present
- Books are Better in Bed
  than Men

GREAT QUOTATIONS, INC.

1967 Quincy Ct. • Glendale Heights, IL 60139

TOLL FREE: 800-354-4889 (outside Illinois)

(708) 582-2800

PRINTED IN HONG KONG